Crushing The Olive Will Release The Oil

The Oil Of His Anointing

Sharmee L. Kemp

I would like to dedicate this book to everyone who has ever found themselves in a crushing process. God wants you to know that the crushing is not in vain He is producing the oil of his anointing out of your pain.

Acknowledgments

I would like to thank all of those who have endured the crushing process with me. I thank you for your willingness to help push me in spite of the obstacles. For everyone who labored, who prayed who called and even just listened during those crushing seasons I would like to thank you. I want to thank a very dear spiritual mother Jane Green who literally labored in prayer with me until she saw Christ being formed in me. I would like to thank my other spiritual parents John and Charlene Burris though you are with the Father your labor is still producing fruit. Constance McNeil, Barbara Ross, Carrie Head, and Apostle Barbara J. McClain love you all more than you know so many days and nights of helping to birth me into who I am now. My friends Sherri, Dawn, and Trish my riders for life thank you all for being you. My sister Nickco and spiritual sister Kathy Parker love you for your labor of love. To my parents Charlie and Gwen Kemp you're always in my heart. My children Kierra, Alex, Sharnee, and Mikhala thank you for loving me through my process.

Table of Contents

Words of Life

- Without breath there is no life
- Without life there is no joy
- Without joy there is no peace
- Without peace there is no Holy Spirit
- Without Holy Spirit there is no Christ Jesus
- Without Christ Jesus there is no God the Father
- Without God the Father there is no breath of life.

Father I ask that every individual who encounters this book would feel a fresh wind of life. I ask you to breathe into their spirit and revive everything that the enemy has declared to be dead. I ask you to go to the deep places and cause your presence to be evident in a way it has not been before in Jesus name I pray.

Sharmee L Kemp

1 WHY THE CRUSHING

Have you ever wondered why at times the walk of faith seems more pressing than other times? If so allow me to take you on a journey that will help you to understand why the pressing is so vital for you to go through. We must understand that whenever there is a pressing it causes something to be released. Now whether that something is oil or not it's up to us to choose.

As previously stated whenever there is a pressing it has come to cause something to be released. Now whether that something produces oil or not God has given us the ability to choose. In life I have gone through many different hardships, many ups and downs and at times it seemed as if I was just riding on a merry go round. There were times in my life when it felt like I was not going to make it, but God has been more than faithful in every situation and circumstance that I have ever found myself in.

Allow me to explain. I was not one who grew up under the word of God, so my foundation from the beginning was not based on Godly principles. I never really understood much about my life until I came into a true intimate relationship with Jesus. Please understand I just don't mean going to church on Sundays and learning all of the right lingo.

I mean the type of relationship where we are allowing God to deal with us behind the scenes where nobody else can go except him and you, where he goes to the core of the things that have harassed and oppressed you for many, many years. Jesus tells us that you shall know the truth and the truth will set you free (John 8:32). We know that where there is freedom there is also much liberty and the one or thing which has had us enslaved has been released off of our lives.

I have learned and I'm still learning that the oil does not come without a price. Now I really want you to understand that when I speak of a price I'm not speaking about money nor am I speaking of a price that can't be paid. We must remember that Jesus already paid the ultimate price for us on Calvary. No, the price that I am speaking of is a price we should all be willing to pay anyway. And that's the price of allowing our flesh to die and allowing Holy Spirit take full control of our lives. The word of God tells us that, your body is the temple of the Holy Spirit, who is in you, whom you received from God. You are not your own, you were brought at a price. Therefore honor God with your body (1 Corinthians 6:19-20).

Now knowing that, it would seem as if we would be overwhelmed with joy to go through the crushing process. Yet, unfortunately many of us are not. Death is never an easy process to endure. Just think about it, in the natural when something or someone dies in our lives it hurts, how much more when we make a choice to put our flesh to death. When we make a decision to kill off our flesh we're also making a decision to pull our emotions in check and to cause them to line up with the word of God. As our flesh begins to die to its own selfish desires our mind will start to align itself with God inspired desires. Our natural man starts to line up with Holy Spirit.

Yet, when we make a decision and we refuse to allow Holy Spirit to put to death things that the old man likes to participate in, it leaves an open door for demonic oppression to come in and invade our lives. They will try to condition us to hold on to the very things that the bible declares will produce death on the inside of us. We stay in bondage to things like anger, bitterness, guilt, shame, rejection, adultery, unforgiveness, envy, fornication, and lying. Yet, we expect to reap fruits of righteousness not realizing that inwardly we are slowly dying.

Now, as we walk around with the things which we did not allow Holy Spirit to destroy, we start to give off a foul odor that is not pleasing to our Father's nostrils. This in turn hinders us from moving into His divine will and plan for our lives. But, when we allow the crushing to take place it produces the oil of God's anointing to flow through us in the power of Holy Spirit. I really want us to understand that I said when we allow which means we have to permit him to do this work within us. We have to be willing to allow the crushing to take place on the inside of us. Now picture this when things are crushed in the natural it gives the appearance of being an excruciating process.

Take a moment and think about the olive, the olive comes in different colors and sizes (just like us), yet it is a perfectly oval shaped type of fruit (we are perfect in the Father's eyes). The olive is a fruit that's best known for the oil that it produces. And in order to get the oil from the olive it must be crushed. But, if the olive is never crushed it remains just a perfectly oval fruit and it was never really used to its full potential. It will never produce the healing elements that can come from the oil that it makes. If the olive just remained an olive the very thing that was in the heart in mind of God was not fulfilled and the olive was never used to its full capacity. I want you to really take a moment and think about that, God created the olive to produce oil. Just as he created us to declare praises to his name (1Peter 2:9).

You can either go through the crushing process downcast in spirit where the enemy of your soul desires for you to be or you can go through with joy the way God intended for you to be (James 1:2). I believe the saddest part of every believer's walk is that many of us never receive the grace that God has given us to walk in while going through the process. Instead of us believing what the word of God has told us in (Isaiah 54:17) that no weapon formed against us will prosper, we would rather believe the lie of the devil when Jesus has already told us that the thief comes to steal, kill, and destroy (John 10:10).

I understand full well that we all go through a time in life where it seems like the enemy is winning, and unfortunately in some of our lives that's very true. The reason why it's true is because we throw in the towel and give up while God is allowing us to walk through things that feel unpleasant to our flesh. Allow me to shed a little more light onto why the process is so important. It helps us to attain Godly character. That's why Paul urges us to persevere in (Romans 5:3-5) and (James1:4) tells us that perseverance must finish its work to become mature in us.

With that being the case we need to come to a place where we are willing to allow God to crush us without giving up in the process. Now please make no mistake about it the crushing will come whether we walk through it with God or whether we walk through it alone. I have personally made the choice to walk through with God and to allow him to mount me up with wings like eagles according to (Isaiah 40:31) and I have chosen not to walk through alone and be in a position to be crushed by the devil.

As I stated in the beginning the choice is ours we can choose life or we can choose death. Father God has made it that simple for every human being. Yet, His desire is that we choose life. That was the purpose for Him giving us his one and only son Jesus. Remember the promises he gave us, "I come that you may have life and have it more abundantly" (John 10:10b) or how about "for this reason was the son of man manifested; that he might destroy the works of the devil" (1 John 3:8). So it really puts the decision back into our hands.

I want you to also understand what's in you comes out of you while you are in the crushing process. The word of God tells us in Luke 6:45 that out of the abundance of the heart the mouth speaks. So while you are going through different testing's in your life; what are some of the things that are flowing from your spirit? I guess the real question would be has the oil that's been coming out of your spirit been pure or defiled? The way that you can answer that is simple. What are some of the things that are being confessed and spoken while going through the place of crushing?

The crushing has come not to hurt us but, to make us into the individuals that God has originally created for us to be. If you stand looking at it from a natural perspective you are going to see things in a different light which is not light at all but darkness. In Proverbs 3:5-6 we are instructed to trust in the Lord with all our hearts and lean not on our own understanding, but in all our ways acknowledge him and he will direct our paths.

Yet, many times we try to figure things out in the natural which causes us to be at a major disadvantage and the enemy of our souls knows that. We must remember that the word declares that the weapons of our warfare are not carnal, but they are mighty in God for the pulling down of strongholds (2 Corinthians 10:4). Then we learn that we wrestle not against flesh and blood, but against the principalities, against powers, against the rulers of the darkness of this age, against spiritual hosts of wickedness in heavenly places (Ephesians 6:10-13).

If that's the case why do we as children of God find it so difficult to believe the word of our heavenly Father? If we will just simply stand on His word we will see the faithfulness of God's word revealed in every step of crushing that we encounter. We will see the crushing was never meant to hurt us but to shape us. We will see the very thing we thought would destroy us is the very thing that's going to help mature us. The crushing is the very thing that will help us to trust in the word of God. But instead of embracing the crushing we wrestle with it because we truly don't believe the one who called us is faithful and he will do it as 1Thessalonians 5:24 declares.

Why is it that during the time of crushing the Lord will allow his word to be released to us, and it seems as if there is more opposition that comes from spiritual darkness because of the Word of the Lord that we received? Why is it that in those times we allow the devil to come and snatch that very word from us? Well I venture to say it's because we really didn't believe that the word we received was from God and that it would truly produce his unshakable life within us. Remember Jesus said I am the way the truth and the life (John 14:6).

So take a moment to think on that fact the very one that has come to give you life has also permitted for you to go through the crushing process. Yet, in His infinite wisdom he knows and understands that it will produce a life of faith, hope, and love on the inside of us. That's only if we allow him to take us through the process so that we may be redeemed for his glory.

We have to be willing to go through it the way that he has predestined for us to go through. We must first agree with the word of God while the crushing is taking place. The word tells us that we were chose and predestined before the creation of the world (Ephesians 1:4-5). We are also told that He knows the thoughts and plans that he thinks towards us, thoughts of good and not evil to give us a hope in our final outcome (Jeremiah 29:11).

We are told that the eyes of the Lord are everywhere keeping watch on the wicked and the good (Proverbs 15:3). Now if the eyes of the Lord are everywhere that means he already knows what we are going through even the demonic that has been permitted to work in our natural situations. Knowing that why do we fear and walk around as though some strange thing is happening to us (1 Peter 4:12-13).

When all we have to do is really decide whose report we're going to believe. The one who comes to leave us hopeless or the one who told us; "I will never leave you nor forsake you" (Hebrews 13:5). For some of us God has permitted the crushing to test us as he brings us to the place of his release. He is testing us so that we may see what's in our hearts as he tested the children of Israel as they walked in their place of wilderness (Deuteronomy 8:2).

I don't want you to be confused about what the Lord has released me to say. This crushing is not the crushing that takes place because of your disobedience or rebellion. I'm talking about the crushing that takes place from the word of the Lord that you received and the enemy has been permitted to touch some things around you because of your agreement with that Word. Now for those of you that are being oppressed because of your unwillingness to submit and walk in the path God has chosen for you. I encourage you to come back in line with the truth of the Lord.

And for those of you who are being crushed and you have been wondering what's going on in your life. You already know who you are because the pure oil has been flowing from your mouth. The Lord wants you to know that he is at work in your life and the crushing has come to release you into a greater level of trust and faith in Him. God has given you his grace and has equipped you with the weapons you need to walk in this place. The Lord told me to tell you to be strong in the Lord and the power of his might.

Don't try to figure this out in the natural for God is making a way in the desert and he is making the crooked places straight. He wants you to know that you shall reap the harvest in due season only don't lose heart and faint allow Him to take you through this place of crushing so that you may receive the reward that only God is able to give you.

The bible declares after you have done all to stand. I want you to know you are not just standing helplessly you are standing in full confidence that the crushing is creating in you a pure heart and it is renewing a right spirit within you according to (Psalms 51:11). The crushing is taking you into a realm in the spirit that you never understood was there until you had to trust God on this level. It is helping you to see what is really down on the inside of you and as (Philippians 4:13) declares, "I can do all things through Christ who gives me strength."

You will find yourself really moving and operating in the grace available to you while the oil is being produced from this time of crushing; oil that is pure and untainted, oil that has been pressed and crushed that it may destroy yolks once it is displayed before men. As you allow the crushing you really do come to a place where you know and understand that crushing the olive really does release the oil and that oil brings about an anointing that will destroy every yolk.

God is looking for us to stay focused and keep our eyes on the goal through the crushing. He wants us to stop allowing life circumstances and situations to choke out his word that has been rooted and grounded in us. We must keep our hearts pure and find ourselves falling more and more at the feet of Jesus. We can't allow the people around us to distract us, but we must stay in the place of which God is requiring of us.

Out of the place of being crushed it is going to produce pure oil and God wants the oil of his anointing to flow from our lives. We must go through the process without bitterness and resentment so that God will cause us to be all that he has ordained for us to be. We will see that although we may have been crushed on every side the Father has provided us a way of escape. We have to remember that our lives are not out in the open, but hidden in Christ and everything that attempts to come our way must first go through the one to whom our lives are hidden in. Rest assured that despite whatever comes our way; it will not prevail according to his word.

2 RELEASING HIS WORSHIP

In this chapter we will discuss the importance of Releasing His Worship during the Crushing Process. You will find that during the crushing your worship means everything. You will come to understand the necessity of giving God that part of you the Devil has always fought to steal since the beginning of time. That part is your worship and that part is on the inside of you.

During times of crushing you will find that your soul (mind, will, and emotions) does not want to line up with the word of the Lord. It will seem as if it is getting harder and harder to lift up your hands as you are going through the crushing process. That's why this chapter is so vital in understanding true worship. Worship is not just done with songs but it's an attitude of heart. The devil would love nothing more than for you to give up and throw in the towel. He would love for you to go through the crushing angry and downcast in heart. Depressed and defeated with a "woe is me" mentality and a compromised spirit.

The main goal of the adversary is to get us to believe there's no hope. And I am fully aware that during times of crushing Satan would like for us to curse God and die as Job wife told him to do in (Job 2:9). Although we may be hard pressed on every side and it may seem as if there's no relief God is still looking for our worship. He is still requiring that we give him pure and undefiled worship the type of worship that's a pleasing aroma unto His nostrils.

I have found and I'm still finding that in the times we feel as if we have lost everything, that our worship means the most. It's in these times where we see that God will truly do what His word has promised. He will give us a garment of praise for a spirit of heaviness as declared in (Isaiah 61:3). I have come to understand that we never get to pick and choose the times and seasons of crushing in our lives nor how long we are to stay in the process.

Our total dependency is on the Lord, which causes us to become broken before him. It's in those times we have to completely abandon the control we thought we had and hand our entire life over to the Father. We find out that in that place the Lord speaks to us and tells us to let go of every desire, heartache, pain, disappointment and surrender all to Him. We find that we are in need of the Lord and not any earthly thing.

I have learned and am still learning that worship is a lifestyle and not just something that's done on Sunday mornings or whenever we come together as a body of believers. True worship comes from our hearts and it's not just lip service. What do we gain if we only worship God with our mouths yet our hearts are far from him? We gain absolutely nothing. As worshippers we must realize that our heart is connected with our speech. If my heart and attitude has not changed during my worship what am I really offering up to God?

The truth of the matter is nothing; let me explain what I mean. If I'm going through different times of testing's, trials, sufferings or tribulations in my life and when I am alone I can't seem to lift up my soul in worship to give God praise thanking him because of who He is and also for where I am I have not yet learned how to be a worshipper at all.

Remember that the word of God tells us that those who worship the Lord will worship him in Spirit and in truth (John 4:24).

Please know and understand that the Spirit of God is always waiting to agree with God and that which he has spoken. As a born again believer our spirit has become new and the bible declares that old things have passed away. So that means the incorruptible seed of God is living on the inside of us. We have to know that it's our flesh that doesn't want us to agree with God. Scripture declares that the Spirit and the flesh are in conflict against one another (Galatians 5:17).

Just understanding that alone causes us to see that our flesh will never want the things of the Spirit so we have to make our fleshly man submit itself to Holy Spirit. Now that's a very key aspect in worship, we have to know that in the times of crushing neither our body nor our soul will feel like worshipping the Lord, so let me repeat what I previously said it's in those times that we have to press in like never before and make our flesh submit itself to Holy Spirit.

We have to move past how we feel and simply do what we know to be true according to the word of God. We are in a day and time where we have believed that worship is done with lip service. Yet, that is far from the truth. Remember Jesus said these people worship me with their mouths, but their hearts are far from me (Matthew 15:8-9). Worship is what we do in spite of obstacles and hardship. We must remember that the way out is through.

Through what you may ask. Through different seasons of crushing's that you may encounter throughout life. We are told in the word of God that we should bless the Lord at all times and his praise shall continuously be on our lips (Psalms 34:1). Tell me what is it that we give to the Lord if we can only bless him when everything is going good in our lives? That would be absolutely nothing, let's look at this for a minute through the eyes of scripture. The word of God tells us to bring unto the Lord a sacrifice of praise (Hebrews 13:15).

But, if I bring to the Lord a sacrifice of praise and I have not yet allowed the Lord to cleanse and purify my heart through the times of crushing that he permits I am at a disadvantage. In the book of Leviticus when a sacrifice is described it is described to us as something that had to first be killed. Bloodshed had to take place in order for anything to be sacrificed to the Lord.

That bloodshed was the way of receiving restitution, and atonement had to be made for the people for whatever sin or sins that was committed. Once the sacrifice was slain according to the word of the Lord it was placed upon the altar and consumed. Think on that for a moment. The same is true with Jesus, he is our ultimate sacrifice his blood has covered all that we would ever do. Now, if it was that way with our Lord it has to be the same way with us, we have to be a living sacrifice unto the Lord. Whenever we give the Lord a sacrifice it has to be dead to us before we can give it and it be a sweet aroma ascending up to Him.

Look at this from the view of Abraham and his son Isaac. The Lord required that Abraham give his son up as a sacrifice. The Lord God said Abraham I want you to sacrifice your only son Isaac to me (Genesis 22:2). Now in order for Abraham to sacrifice his son of promise I venture to say that he had to consider Isaac dead to him in order for him to be willing to give Isaac up as a sacrifice.

I would like for us to take a moment and ponder that thought. Whenever we bring the Lord a sacrifice we have to make a decision in our hearts that whatever we sacrifice to Him it has to be dead to us. A worshipper must come to a place where he or she understands that. It is impossible for us to truly present something to the Lord without us first putting it to death. When we don't we find ourselves giving off a foul odor unto God.

We have to grab a hold to that truth. When something is not considered dead it means that it's still alive. Whenever we try to give the Lord something that has not been sacrificed we are prone to take it back from him. So now we see why the death of our sacrifices is so important before we are able to give the Lord a true sacrifice of praise. Once the death has taken place we give the Father the right away to take full control of everything in our lives. Please understand worship is not just a song that we sing it's a lifestyle that we bring unto the Lord.

True worship is agreeing with what the Lord has already spoken. Allow me to repeat what I just said true worship is agreeing with what the Spirit of the Lord has already uttered. It's coming in agreement with the word of the Lord and his faithfulness. True worship brings us in line with Holy Spirit it causes us to see things from God's point of view. It brings us into a place of intercession which produces joy, peace, and the glory of the Lord. True worship causes us not to be moved by natural circumstances and situations you see above them and not beneath them.

You see by the spirit of the Lord and not by the things of the flesh. In this place of worship we truly learn how to abound like Paul did which was in whatever state he found himself in. Whether in need or having plenty well fed or hungry living in plenty or want Paul knew how to abound in every circumstance and situation. He found out that he was able to do all things through Christ who gives him strength (Philippians 4:12-13). That's the place of worship the Lord wants for all of his children.

David said it best in (Psalms 51:17) that a broken spirit and contrite heart the Lord will not despise.

So we see that in order to be a worshiper we have to first be broken. Some of us can become humble out of a place of brokenness. I want you to notice something. I said some of us and not all and that's because, for some no matter how we are crushed we are still determined to do things our own way. But, for those who are willing to release pure worship in spite of what's been launched at you just rest assured that in due season the Lord will promote you. The word of the Lord declares that he resist the proud, but exalts the humble (1 Peter 5:5-6).

The Lord will increase you into such a place in him that everything that you face will have to bow down to the name of Jesus. We are told in (Psalms 20:1) that the name of the God of Jacob will protect us. We must remember that the name of the Lord is a strong tower the righteous run into it and they are saved (Proverbs 18:10). Understand that worship brings us into the presence of the Lord. It brings us right to the throne room of the Father where it's just him and us and he is able to speak directly to our hearts. He gives us what we are in need of and that's Him!

During the time of crushing we have to not allow our worship to come out of a place of duty. It should never be done on the basis that we are supposed to do it. Worship should come out of a place of true devotion unto the Lord. A place of being sold out to the one who is shaping and forming our character through the crushing process. Our worship should overflow with love and gratitude just like Mary Magdalene picture her as she pours out the oil from her alabaster box.

She worshipped Jesus from the heart. A woman who the bible says had seven demons cast out of her. She knew what it was like to go through places and it seems as if no one understands, but she meets the one who truly did Jesus himself. True worship is birthed out of loving God with all your heart and all your soul.

A worshipper understands no matter what crumbles around them their life is not their own and the reason that they live is to worship Him. A worshipper is able to stand on the word of the Lord in the midst of whatever crushing the Lord has permitted for them to go through. The word declares to us He who promised is faithful and he will do it (Hebrews 10:3). Worship is never based just upon a feeling true worship is based on intimate fellowship with the one who has called you into righteousness.

A worshipper is one that who can face life circumstances head on and still declare Lord I trust you no matter what crushing process you allow me to go through. He or she is one who can say what Job said, "though you slay me, yet I will trust you". Then we have David who the bible declares went and worshiped the Lord after the loss of his child. Now that place of worship had to be a heart connection. Neither Job nor David allowed their emotions to dictate the outcome of their worship. They did not allow the tragic circumstances in their lives to override what had been embedded in their hearts.

I know for many in times of crushing worship will not be the first thing on our minds. But that's the time to push past how we feel and press into God. We must realize that our walk is not based on a feeling. We will never just feel like giving God worship because the flesh is weak. Our flesh always wants to gravitate to that which is comfortable and easy. Yet, when we choose to walk in ease we lose the comfort of being wrapped in the Father's arms. So we are to never give into our fickle emotions. We can't trust them for one second they will always lead us astray.

We have to put our focus on the Lord and in the power of His word. He already gave us the promise that the battle was not ours, but it was his (2 Chronicles 20:15). I really can't express enough on how vital it is for us to release our worship to the Lord in the midst of the crushing. Your worship is what makes the crushing process endurable. Worship changes the heart of man and it causes us to look at things according to the supernatural realm and not the natural. It helps us to come to a place where we agree with the Lord and we stop trying to figure out our circumstances from a natural view point.

In times of worship we really do receive the mind of the Lord and as we keep our mind on Him he keeps us in perfect peace (Isaiah 26:3). When you release the worship that God has ordained you keep the enemy at bay his lies and mental assaults are cast to the wayside. The power of worship is to help you while in the crushing it helps you to guard the word that God has spoken over your life like Paul admonished young Timothy to do. This place of worship is the type of worship that really does releases faith in the realm of the supernatural. It's the type of worship that you no longer see your obstacles as unbeatable, but obtainable. This worship keeps your heartbeat in sync with the heart of the Father. This type of worship causes the oil to be released all the more from your life.

True worship release you into another dimension in your understanding and communication with the Lord. The type of worship that is pure and undefiled, holy and true. This is the type of worship that the Father looks for. We have to understand that if we don't release our worship to the Father we are still releasing worship. It's just simply being released to the one the bible calls the Father of lies (Satan). He would love nothing more than to have our worship. Well you may ask "how can I worship the devil"? The answer is simple the unbelief of our heart and the words that we have allowed to come out our mouth during times of crushing's.

Satan plays on our words and if he can convince us to speak things contrary to what the Word of God has declared he has already defeated us into worshipping him. Our words really do depict how we worship. The things that flow from our mouth are a good indicator of what we worship. When we come to a place that we understand that God is the potter and we are the clay he will be able to mold us into the men and women that he desires for us to be.

The Father's desire for us is that we become all that he has predestined and purposed in his heart. His heart is for his children to express their love and affection in whatever state we find ourselves in. He wants us to learn to worship him in the fullness of his Holiness. We are told that those that worship the Lord will worship him in Spirit and in truth. God has created all creation to worship Him. He is never going to be without honor; because of the majestic being that He is he deserves our worship. Yet, God has given us the choice to worship Him that's one of man's most powerful tools the tool of choice. He has given that to every individual in life and he will not go against what he has already established here on earth.

We can make the choice to worship Him from a pure heart or choose to worship Satan from a sinful unbelieving heart. The choice is ours; he said I lay before you this day life and death you choose. He has given us the ability to allow Jesus to be glorified in our lives or not he has never forced anything upon mankind. He will never make us bow down and worship him while we are walking the earth.

We have to come to a place that we release full control of our lives to the Lord and allow Holy

Spirit to take over. The bible declared that Jesus grew in grace and he was full of Holy Spirit. I believe that is true for every born again believer. We are also told that these things were written for our learning /instruction. He wants us to come to a place where we are sure that we are able to handle whatever we may face in life.

It is vital for us to do this with a trusting confidence in Him knowing that he has a way regardless of what our circumstances may say. A worshipper understands that God is moving even when it can't be seen with the natural eye. We have to understand that He is working all things after the counsel of His will.

Worship draws us into intimacy with the Father it causes us to come into a place of rest and security. Untainted worship will lead you into a place of prophetic intercession. Please know that worship and intercession goes hand in hand you can't have one without the other. Once you have released your worship the Lord speaks. He will begin to show you things that are close and dear to His heart. Holy Spirit will even do as Jesus told us in His word; he will remind us of things which are to come (John 16:13).

A worshipper understands that no matter what's going on that God has the solutions that are needed. He or she knows that the Lord is working on their character and they allow God to do his perfect work inside of them. A worshipper is one who has comprehended that the weapons of their warfare are not carnal but they are mighty in God for the pulling down of strongholds (2 Corinthians 10:3-6). He or she knows that if God does not do another thing for them he has already done more than enough. These are the ones that know that it's about the glory of the Lord being revealed in and through them.

They are ones that are not intimidated by others nor the voice of the enemy. They have a loving confidence in the one who has called them by their name. The one who has stood and fought their battles in every other situation they faced in life. They have come to the conclusion that their lives are hidden in Christ Jesus and not just out in the open.

Worshippers can't be stopped and the enemy knows that! He knows every time you open up your mouth that the oil of God's anointing is being released. The oil that will break chains of bondage and tear down kingdoms.

It's the anointing that the bible declares will destroy yolks. And every time you stand in a posture of worship the devil knows that bondages are being destroyed. So his main goal is to stop your worship to stop you from opening your mouth from a pure heart. He knows that the oil of your praise is worth much more than any earthly thing we can obtain. Satan knows that your heart has been connected to the Father. So if he can get you to believe that God is not faithful in the time of crushing he knows you will not posture yourself for worship.

Satan goal is to get you to start blaming yourself, others and God. He wants your thoughts to become so real to you that releasing worship will be the farthest thing from your mind. We must come to a place where we really obtain the habit of keeping our minds stayed on Jesus. A place that we allow the peace of God to dwell in us richly as the word has declared so we may know the hope of glory that's down on the inside of us. One of the things that we have to be careful about is declaring the word without the Spirit of the Lord behind it.

Remember the letter kills and the Spirit gives life (2 Corinthians 3:6). So while you are going through times of crushing if your heart is not connected to the words that are being released the Father knows because your words are your greatest indicator of what's going on in the heart. As it was already stated it's out of the abundance of the heart that the mouth will speak.

Let's look at the Jewish leaders in Jesus day they were great scholars of the law yet the spiritual side was a blare to them. They lacked so much understanding into spiritual things that Jesus called them blind guides. As sad as that was it is still happening in our lives today. Our understanding of spiritual principles is based on things taught by man and their experience instead of the Word of the Lord and the Spirit that he declared will give us life. We do not and will not obtain the promises of God based on worldly knowledge because the Word declares that knowledge puffs up (1 Corinthians 8:1).

We have to make a conscience choice and decision that God deserves our worship. It has to be intentional and on purpose. It has to be a place that our hearts have agreed with whatever process that God has put before us. When we decide to give the Lord our worship we see Satan trembling at the knees. He knows that worship is man's greatest weapon against him and the thing that connects us to God's heart. Remember he was the one who gathered the worship and presented it to the Lord according to scripture. So because of that he will cause all the ammunition he has to be launched at us. So that we may hold back our worship. He wants nothing more than for it to be impure and tainted like him.

Yet, regardless to the ammunition that the enemy throws our way the more our hearts need to bow down in worship to our King. The more we praise the closer we come to seeing the glory of the Lord revealed in our situations. The crushing becomes less noticeable because our focus is on Jesus. The same is true the other way around, the more that we find ourselves having pity parties the more we become closer to Satan. If you would like victory you must stay in a posture of worship while you are in the crushing. If you choose to operate from a place of defeat continue to praise whatever mountain you are facing.

One of the things we must realize is the crushing has not taken God by surprise. God knows exactly what we are going through and the steps we need to take as we go through the process. We must keep our eyes on the Lord and not allow the crushing to keep us from releasing our worship to Him. We must understand that God has a plan and if you desire to see the finished work of that which He has in store for you. Stay on the path He has set before you regardless to how difficult the crushing may seem at the moment.

We have to know that all things are working together for the good of those that are called according to his purpose (Romans 8:28). All we have to do is have a trusting assurance in Him knowing that He is working a lasting foundation within us. I want us to know that God is looking for our worship. He is looking for a people that will be willing to give all their devotion to Him in the midst of the crushing, He is looking for you and He is looking for me.

He is requiring that we come up higher in our thinking. He is looking to increase our understanding about who He is. We have to allow Holy Spirit to teach us how to worship our creator so that we may truly be one in heart and mind with Him the Father never wanted for us to feel helpless in the times of crushing. He wanted us to know the freedom that comes from within when we learn how to worship while we are in this place. He is looking to mend that which has been broken by man before we ever came into the saving knowledge of His grace.

He is looking for us to stay focused and to keep our eyes on the goal. And stop allowing life circumstances and situations to choke his word that was rooted on the inside of us. We must keep our hearts pure and ourselves falling more and more at His feet, but we must stay in the place of crushing that God is requiring of us. For out of the place of being crushed it is going to produce the oil and God wants the oil to flow from our lives.

He wants us to know what it really means to worship in spirit and in truth. He is looking for us to lay it all down before Him and see his hand move among us in ways we can't even imagine. He wants us to bring to him that sacrifice of praise. That praise when we kill everything that's keeping our flesh alive.

He is looking for a crucifying of the flesh. He wants to know if we are willing to put to death those things that are robbing us of our worship to Him. He wants our thank offerings and He wants to hear our songs of worship that our heart speaks when we are worshipping Him. He wants to know that he has our undivided attention and that everything else fails in comparison to Him. So I leave you with this: A time of crushing should always lead us into a place of worship a place where the oil of the anointing released off of our life is a sweet smelling fragrance to the Father.

I pray that we will make a decision to trust Him regardless to where we may find ourselves and know He is still looking for us to come to Him. He told us to come to me all who are heavy laden take my yoke upon you and learn from me for my yoke is easy and my burdens are light and we will find rest for our souls (Matthew 11:28-29). Worship will put our souls at rest because we have come to Him.

Worship is a learned behavior it's a condition of the heart. As we position our hearts to worship the Lord we operate in a place of adoration unto the Lord. True worship offers unhindered praise. Simply thinking of the goodness of the Lord will always cause a true worshipper to lift up their hands and start declaring how awesome the Creator God is no matter the circumstance they find themselves in. God finds a true worshipper in all of us if we are willing to simply submit ourselves to the cross of the Lord. As we do that we will see that though we are crushed on ever side God has placed in us the tools we need to worship Him.

I pray as you have taken the opportunity to read this that you would understand the power that lies within you to go through the crushing process, and to lift up not only your hands, but your hearts in worship. I pray that you would allow God to crush you in the areas that He desires. That you may be a Trophy for God's Glory that you will enter into realms that you have never thought possible. And allow the power of Holy Spirit to transform you in such a way that your very presence will effect change in others.

3 PROPHETIC DECLARATION

Father I declare that I am a child of the King. I declare that I am able to do all things though Christ who gives me strength. I declare that I walk and flow in all heavenly gifts. I declare that my feet are like hinds feet and I will leap on my high places. I declare that I am full of the Holy Spirit in accordance to your word. I declare that the enemy is under my feet and I walk and move in the supernatural. I declare that I have an abundance of increase and wealth is my portion. I declare that my household is blessed and producing fruit on a daily basis. I declare that my finances are overflowing. I declare I am in good health and my mind is filled with the trea-sures of your word. I declare that no weapon that is formed against me is going to prosper, because according to your word I am the head and not the tail. I declare that everything around me is mov-ing under the power and authority of your word because I am a royal priesthood. I declare that chains are being broken in the atmosphere all around me because the anointing on my life is so thick that it cuts asunder. I declare that men are pouring into my bosom on a day to day basis by the authority of your word. I declare that wisdom is my best friend and understanding is my closest kin. I declare that the chains of wickedness are broken and bondages or no longer in operation in my life. I declare that greater is He in me than he that is in this world. I declare that I have the mind of Christ Jesus and all goodness and mercy will follow me. I declare that sickness and disease has no place in me because according to your word I am healed by your stripes. I declare that I am reaping the harvest of plenty because my seeds are being sown on good ground. I declare that I am blessed in the city and in the field. I declare that my store houses are full. I declare that I am a generous giver. I declare that I am living to my full potential and signs and wonders are following me. I declare that the angels of the Lord are encamped around me and they are protecting me. I declare that I am rooted and grounded in faith. I declare that my love walk is expanding to others and my life is impacting change in the earth.

4 PRAYER

Father I thank you that I am excelling in all
areas of my life. I thank you that I am be-
coming more and more like you with each increasing day. I thank you that I have victory in every
aspect of my life. I thank you that I am operating
and moving forward in all areas that pertain to
my walk with you.

I thank you that I have a spirit of motivation
and advancement and everything that was stag-
nated and dead has been awakened by the power
and anointing of your word. I thank you that my
body is operating at its full potential and every
aspect of my life has lined up with your word.

I thank you that I am not just a hearer but a
doer of your word. I thank you that you are puri-
fying my heart before you because you are show-
ing me the hidden things of dishonesty that's on

the inside of me. I thank you that my level of maturity is increasing because I am no longer being conformed to the pattern of this world. I thank you that you are pushing me into my destiny because my heart chooses to follow you and you said there's no good thing that you would withhold from me.

I thank you that you are producing much fruit in me because I have chosen to eat on your word day and night. I thank you that my desires for righteousness is increasing because you said that if I hunger and thirst for righteousness I would be filled. I thank you that I am moving at the pace that you require for me to move in and I am not moving ahead of you nor behind you because I am walking in step with the Holy Ghost.

I thank you that I am able to pull down and demolish strongholds according to your word. I thank you that your name is a strong tower and I can run into it and find safety. I thank you that you have given me the ability to walk by faith and not by sight. I thank you that I am able to stand fully clothed in the armor of God according to your word.

I thank you that I am seated in heavenly places in Christ Jesus. Father I thank you that my love for you is deepening because you told me if I seek you I shall find you. I thank you that I am in full operation of understanding spiritual things.

I thank you that am stepping into purpose and destiny because your word tells me that you know the thoughts and plans that you think towards me are thoughts of good and not evil to give me a future and a hope. I thank you that you are helping me to become established in truth because the word tells me to lean not to my own understanding but in all my ways I should acknowledge you and allow you to direct my paths. I thank you that my faith is being increased daily.

I thank you that the word tells me that he who promised is faithful and that you will do all that you have promised to do for me according to your word because it is your word that will not return back void. I thank you Father that you are helping me to obtain everything that pertains to holiness and righteousness.

I thank you that I am making right decisions and living in obedience to your word. I thank you that the spirit of compromise is far from me and that I am able to discern between good and evil by the ability of the Holy Ghost. Father I thank you that I am flourishing like a tree that's planted by the rivers of water. And I give you praise and honor for it now in Jesus name. Amen

About the Author

Sharmee Kemp is a teacher, writer radio and television host, a speaker and she's the founder of Trophies for God's Glory. Her home town is St. Louis MO and she is the mother of four wonderful children Kierra, Sharnee, Mikhala, Alex and has several beautiful grandchildren who keeps her on her toes.

The Lord has anointed Sharmee to operate in the gift of Intercession and Deliverance. Through this gifting He has manifested his healing anointing, his delivering power and the gift of prophecy to flow effectively through her. He has caused her to birth Trophies for God's Glory where the emphasis is on being set free. She is a multi talented individual who God is raising up to help advance his Kingdom in these end times.

The Lord has empowered Sharmee the ability to walk in a Romans 12:2 anointing where the focus is being transformed by the renewing of the mind. The Lord has so graciously released this yoke crushing anointing on her after He delivered her from mental illness over 15 years ago and helped her to transform her mind by his word. Her heart's desire is to see all mankind healed, delivered and set free from the clutches and enslavement of the enemy.

Father God has laid it heavy upon her heart to see all born-again believers, non-believers and back sliders walking in their God-given destiny and purpose for their lives. He has allowed her to use these gifts to disciple others that they in turn my go out and make disciples. So through a place of prayer and studying of the word He allows her to activate her talents into the lives of others, that they may live a life that is filled with love, grace, hope, peace and abundance through our Lord Jesus Christ.

Made in United States
Orlando, FL
03 February 2022

14380545R00039